IN DEFENSE OF SAINT CYPRIAN

WITH REFERENCE TO ST. NIKODEMOS AND *THE RUDDER*

St. Raphael of Brooklyn

In Defense of Saint Cyprian

with Reference to St. Nikodemos
and *The Rudder*

Saint Raphael of Brooklyn

Uncut Mountain Press

IN DEFENSE OF SAINT CYPRIAN

with Reference to St. Nikodemos and *The Rudder*

uncutmountainpress.com

Special thanks to Maher Salloum.

Scriptural quotations are emended to better reflect the original text.

Saint Raphael (Hawaweeny) of Brooklyn, 1860–1915.

In Defense of St. Cyprian: with Reference to St. Nikodemos and *The Rudder*.—1ˢᵗ ed.

ISBN: 978-1-63941-034-7

I. Orthodox Christian History
II. Orthodox Christian Ecclesiology

St. Cyprian of Carthage

فهرس المحتويات

TABLE OF CONTENTS

الفصل المائتان والحادي والأربعون
عماد الهراطقة ومجلة المشرق اليسوعية
العدد ٨ ، ١٥ نيسان ١٩١٠ ، السنة السادسة، ص ١٤١ – ١٥٤

كنا قد عقدنا مقالة روحية في العدد الـ ٢٢ من سنة مجلتنا ١٩٠٩ المنقضية ضمّناها مختصر تاريخ المجامع التسعة المكانية المثبتة قوانينها من المجامع المسكونية وقد وضعناها بحسب تاريخ انعقادها، وأقدمها المجمع الذي انعقد في مدينة قرطجنة تحت رئاسة أسقفها القديس الشهيد كبريانوس في سنة ٢٥٦. وقلنا إن هذا المجمع أصدر رسالة قانونية تُسمّى قانوناً وتأمر بوجوب تعميد الهراطقة المرتدّين إلى الكنيسة الجامعة أرثوذكسية، وقد اعترف به وثبّته أولاً المجمع الثاني المسكوني في قانونه السابع وذلك ضمناً كما سنرى، وثانياً المجمع السادس المسكوني في قانونه الثاني وذلك صريحاً بذكره اسم الرسالة القانونية

IN DEFENSE OF
SAINT CYPRIAN[1]

from *The Orthodox Word*

We had published a spiritual article in the 22nd issue of the year 1909 of our magazine, in which we included a summary of the history of the Nine Local Councils whose canons were ratified by the Ecumenical Councils, and we presented them according to the date of their convening. The oldest among them is the Council that convened in the city of Carthage, presided by its bishop, Saint Cyprian the Martyr, in the year 256. The council issued a canonical letter, called a canon, and commanded that heretics reverting to the Catholic Orthodox Church should be baptized, and this was implicitly recognized and ratified by, first, the Second Ecumenical Council in its seventh canon, as we shall see, and second, by the Sixth Ecumenical Council in its second canon, explicitly by mentioning the name of the canonical

1   *The Orthodox Word*, Issue 8, April 15 1910, 6th Year, pp. 141-155. Found in *The Complete Works of Saint Raphael of Brooklyn* (in Arabic), Tome 2, Chapter 241.

ونسبتها إلى القديس كبريانوس ومجمعه المذكور آنفاً.

فتناولنا مؤخراً العدد الأخير أي العدد الثاني من مجلة "المشرق" اليسوعية البيروتية لسنتها ١٩١٠ الحاضرة، وإذا فيه مقالة عنوانها "عماد الهراطقة ومجلة الكلمة الأرثوذكسية" زعم حضرة كاتبها أولاً كون مجمع قرطجنة الذي انعقد في سنة ٢٥٦ والذي وضعته مجلتنا في مقدمة المجامع المكانية التسعة المثبتة من المجامع المسكونية لا صحة له حتى عند الكنيسة الأرثوذكسية أيضاً وذلك لأن حضرته لم يجد له ذكراً في جميع ما اتصلت إليه يده من المجموعات العربية الأرثوذكسية المطبوعة، والمخطوطة وثانياً كون القانون السابع للمجمع الثاني المسكوني ليس فقط لا يثبت مجمع قرطجنة هذا بل بالحري يخالفه، وكون القانون الثاني للمجمع السادس المسكوني الذي يذكر صريحاً رسالة كبريانوس ومجمعه القانونية هو "من جملة قوانين ليست للمجمع السادس المسكوني لكنها لمجمع القبة (ترولّو) الذي ألحقه اليونان سراً بالمجمع المسكوني دون اتفاق الآباء، ولا تزال الكنيسة الكاثوليكية تنكر قانونيته إذ لم يثبته الأحبار الرومانيون"!

قلنا وما كان أغنى مجلة "المشرق" عن هذا التحكك الآخر بمجلتنا "الكلمة" وبما نثبته فيها من تعاليم كنيستنا واعتقاداتها

letter and attributing it to Saint Cyprian and his Council previously mentioned.

We were recently grappling with the last issue, i.e., the second issue of the Jesuit Beirut magazine *Al-Mashreq* (*The Orient*) of its present year 1910, in which there was an article entitled "The Baptism of Heretics and the *Orthodox Word* Magazine" whose "honorable" author first claimed that the Council of Carthage that took place in the year 256 (and which our magazine had placed at the forefront of the Nine Local Councils that have been confirmed by the Ecumenical Council) has no validity even for the Orthodox Church as well! That is because his "excellency" did not find it mentioned in all the printed and handwritten Arabic Orthodox collections that he could obtain. Second, he claims that the seventh canon of the Second Ecumenical Council, not only does not ratify this Council of Carthage, but rather contradicts it; and that the fact that the second canon of the Sixth Ecumenical Council, which explicitly mentions the letter of Saint Cyprian and his Canonical Council, is among "a number of canons that do not belong to the Sixth Ecumenical Council, but to the Dome Council (of Trullo)[2], which the Greeks secretly appended to the Ecumenical Council without the agreement of the Fathers, and whose legitimacy is still denied by the Catholic Church as it was not ratified by the Roman Popes!"

We say that *Al-Mashreq* magazine could have spared itself this clash with our magazine *The Orthodox Word* and what we prove in it of the teachings and beliefs of our Church.

---

2   The Council in Trullo or Trullan Council, also known as the Fifth-Sixth Council, Quinisext Council, or the Penthekte Synod, was held at Constantinople under Justinian II in 692. The "Council in Trullo" derives its name from being held in a domed hall in the Imperial Palace (τροῦλος, meaning dome or cup).

سواءٌ كانت الكنائس المسيحية الأخرى الغير الأرثوذكسية تسلم بها
أو لا تسلم فهذا لا يهمنا، بل ما يهمنا هو تعليم شعبنا الأرثوذكسي
اعتقادات كنيستنا المسلَّمة إليها من الرسل الأطهار وآباء المجامع
السبعة المسكونية الأبرار ليس إلا.

وإذا كنا لدى ذكرنا ما تعتقد به كنيستنا نذكر أحياناً أيضاً ما لا تعتقد
به فما قصدنا بذلك إلا زيادة الايضاح وليس فتح أبواب مناظرات دينية
عقيمة لا فائدة منها ولا جدوى إن لم نقل إنها مضرة بالأحرى. وهذا
ما جعلنا لدى كلامنا عن "عصمة الكنيسة في مجامعها المسكونية
المقدسة" (انظر العدد الـ ٢١ من سنة مجلتنا المنقضية صفحة ٤٠١ -
٤٠٥) نغفل ذكر عقيدة حديثة وضعتها الكنيسة الباباوية في سنة ١٨٧٠
وهي عقيدة "عصمة البابا" التي أضحكتنا ملاحظة صاحب المقالة في
"المشرق" بشأنها إذ قال: "وقد جعل الكاتب (أي نحن) العصمة في
الكنيسة بمعزل عن الرأس خليفة بطرس نائب الرسل ويعني به بابا
رومية" حالة كونه يعرف جيداً أن كنيستنا الأرثوذكسية لم تعترف قط
بما أحدثه باباوات رومية من التعاليم والعقائد الغريبة قبل انفصال
كنيستهم الغربية عن كنائس المشرق الأرثوذكسية، فكيف ينتظر منا
ونحن أحد أبناء كنيسة المسيح الأرثوذكسية أن نعترف له بعصمة البابا
التي لما ابتدعتها كنيسته في الجيل الماضي قد اضطر بسببها عشرات
الألوف من الكاثوليك في أوروبة أن يخرجوا من حظيرة الكنيسة الباباوية
ويؤلِّفوا كنيسة مستقلة تحت اسم "كنيسة الكاثوليك القدماء" أي
المحافظين على تعليم الكنيسة القديم؟ إن في ملاحظته هذه المنتهى
الغرابة فنحن كنا ولا نزال نبذل جهد المستطاع في سبيل تجنب ذكر كل
ما من شأنه مسّ حاسيات بقية أخوتنا المسيحيين الغير الأرثوذكسيين
ولا سيما التعرض لما تنشره محلاتهم وصحفهم من التعاليم

Whether the other non-Orthodox Christian churches accept them or not, this does not concern us. What concerns us is solely teaching our Orthodox people the beliefs of our Church as handed [to us] by the Holy Apostles and the Righteous Fathers of the Seven Ecumenical Councils.

And if, while mentioning what our church believes, we sometimes also mention what it does not believe, we only do so for a better clarification, not to open the doors to sterile religious debates that are useless and futile, not to mention rather harmful. This is what made us, when we spoke about "the infallibility of the Church in her Holy Ecumenical Councils" (see the 21st issue of the previous year, pages 401-405), avoid mentioning a new doctrine established by the Papal Church in the year 1870, which is the doctrine of "the Infallibility of the Pope," where the comment of the article's author in *Al-Mashreq* made us laugh. He said: "And the writer (i.e., us) made the infallibility in the Church separate from the head, the successor of Peter, the vicar of the Apostles, (meaning the Pope of Rome.)" Knowing very well that our Orthodox Church never recognized the strange teachings and beliefs introduced by the Roman Popes that preceded the schism of their Western Church from the Eastern Orthodox Churches, how does he expect us, the children of the Orthodox Church of Christ, to acknowledge to him the infallibility of the Pope, which, when his Church invented it during the last generation, forced tens of thousands of Catholics in Europe to leave the fold of the Papal Church and form an independent church under the name of the "Old Catholics' Church," that is, the keepers of the ancient teaching of the Church? This observation of his is extremely strange, for we were, and still are, making every possible effort in order to avoid mentioning anything that would offend the sensibilities of the rest of our non-Orthodox Christian brothers, especially meddling in what their shops and newspapers publish about their own teachings

والعقائد الخاصة بهم، في حين أن مجلة "المشرق" الكاثوليكية قد
آلت على نفسها ولا سيما منذ ظهور مجلة "النعمة" البطريركية
الأرثوذكسية إلا التحرش بنا وبمجلتنا (ويكتب لنا منشورة منذ ثماني
عشرة سنة!) ولا سيما في مواضيع لم نتعرّض فيها لذكر كنيستها بشيء
البتة، كموضوع تعليم كنيستنا "الأسفار الغير القانونية" وموضوع
"المجامع التسعة المكانية" التي تعتبرها كنيستنا اعتبار المجامع
السبعة المسكونية المقدسة وما شاكل. ومع أنا نكره الدخول في
مناظرات دينية أو كنائسية مع من هم ليسوا على مذهبنا ولا من
كنيستنا، وذلك لأن الاختبار علمنا أن أمثال هذه المناظرات تكون على
الغالب وخيمة العواقب وتضرّ أكثر مما تنفع لم نر مع ذلك مندوحة
من الجواب بكل اختصار على مقالة "المشرق" الأخيرة بشأن المجمع
الأول المكاني المقدس وقراره بوجوب تعميد الهراطقة لكي لا يظن
صاحبها نفسه حكيماً فينتفخ وعالماً بتعاليم الكنيسة الأرثوذكسية
واعتقاداتها أكثر من الأرثوذكسيين أنفسهم فيعثر ويعثر الآخرين.

فأولاً:

قال صاحب المقالة في "المشرق" رداً على قولنا "إن في الكنيسة
الأرثوذكسية تسعة مجامع مكانية قديمة مثبتة من المجامع المقدسة
المسكونية ولهذا تعتبر معصومة عن الغلط وأولها المجمع المكاني
المنعقد في قرطجنة سنة ٢٥٥-٢٥٦ الخ"، كون "الكنيسة الأرثوذكسية
لم تتفق على هذا العدد فقد ذكر بعضهم عشرة مجامع مكانية وغيرهم
تسعة أو سبعة الخ وعليه يحتاج قول الكلمة إلى نظر".

and beliefs, while the Catholic magazine *Al-Mashreq* has committed itself, especially since the appearance of the Orthodox Patriarchal magazine *Al-Ne'mah* (*The Grace*), to harass us and our magazine (in addition to books that we have published eighteen years ago!), particularly on issues where we never mentioned its church at all, such as the topic of our church's teaching of the "Apocryphal Books" and the topic of the "Nine Local Councils" which our church reckons as being of the same standing as the Seven Holy Ecumenical Councils, and so forth. Although we dislike engaging in religious or ecclesiastical debates with those who do not share our doctrines and do not belong to our Church, because experience has taught us that such debates often have dire consequences and do more harm than good, we had no choice but briefly replying to *Al-Mashreq's* last article on the First Holy Local Council and its decision concerning the necessity of baptizing the heretics, so that its author does not think of himself as wise and puffed up, thinking that he is knowledgeable of the teachings and beliefs of the Orthodox Church more than the Orthodox themselves, thus becoming a stumbling block to himself and others.

First:

In response to our statement that "there are Nine Ancient Local Councils in the Orthodox Church, confirmed by the Holy Ecumenical Councils, and for this reason they are considered infallible, the first among them is the Local Council held in Carthage in the year 255-256, etc…", the author of the article in *Al-Mashreq* said, "the Orthodox Church did not agree on this number, as some of them mentioned ten Local Councils, and others nine or seven, etc. Therefore, what *The Word* mentioned needs re-consideration."

أما نحن فنجيبه:

إن قول "الكلمة" بكون المجامع المكانية المثبتة من المجامع المقدسة المسكونية هي تسعة هو قول كنيستنا الأرثوذكسية الرسمي أي رأي الكنيسة الأرثوذكسية جمعاء المدوَّن في كتبها الرسمية المثبتة أو المعترف بها رسمياً من جميع رؤساء الكنائس الأرثوذكسية بدون استثناء، وليس في كتب مترجمة قديماً أو حديثاً ومخطوطة أو مطبوعة بدون مصادقة رسمية. فحضرة صاحب المقالة في "المشرق" - كما يعترف هو نفسه - لم يصل إلى يده من الكتب المطبوعة والمخطوطة بشأن المجامع المقدسة إلا نحو أربعة أو خمسة من الكتب المخطوطة بالعربية، فضلاً عن كتابين مطبوعين **أحدهما** يُسمى كتاب "الكنز الثمين" نقله عن الروسية إلى العربية جميل أفندي انطاكي وطبعه في سنة ١٩٠٧ وهو عبارة عن كتاب تعليمي في أصول الحقوق الكنائسية وليس مجموعة جميع قوانين الرسل والآباء والمجامع المسكونية والمكانية **والثاني** هو "كتاب" قوانين الرسل والمجامع المسكونية والمكانية" مطبوع من شخص مجهول في مطبعة المحروسة بمصر سنة ١٨٩٤ عن ترجمة خطية لأحد بطاركة الشرق مجهول الاسم والتفسير فيها اتخذه هذا البطريرك المجهول عن بطريرك آخر شرقي مجهول أيضاً! وهذا الكتاب الأخير الذي مترجمه ومفسر قوانينه وناشره طبعاً مجهولون وغير مصادق عليه حتى ولا من رئاسة إحدى الكنائس الأرثوذكسية لا يزيد اعتباره عن اعتبار بقية المجموعات العربية المحفوظة خطأً وفيها ما فيها كما لا يخفى من الغلطات والتحريفات من النساخ والاختصارات في عدد المجامع والقوانين. ولهذا لا يجوز لمن يدعي العلم والمعرفة أن يستند إلى مثل هذه الكتب الغير الرسمية في إثبات حقيقة أو دحضها بل عليه أن يلجأ إلى الكتب الرسمية المنشورة طبعاً

As for us, we answer him:

The Word's statement, that there are nine Local councils confirmed by the Holy Ecumenical Councils, is the official statement of our Orthodox Church, i.e., the opinion of the entire Orthodox Church that is recorded in her official books that are confirmed or officially recognized by all the Heads of the Orthodox Churches without exception, and not in books translated in the past or in modern times that are handwritten or printed without official endorsement. The author of the article in *Al-Mashreq*—as he himself admits—could not access any printed and handwritten books on the Holy Councils except about four or five handwritten books in Arabic, in addition to two printed books, **one** of which is called *The Precious Treasure* which was translated from Russian into Arabic by Jamil Effendi Antaqi, and printed in the year 1907, and which is an educational book on the fundamentals of ecclesiastical laws, not a collection of all the canons of the Apostles, the Fathers, and the Ecumenical and Local councils. **The second** is the *Book of Canons of the Apostles and Ecumenical and Local Councils* printed by an unknown person in Al-Mahrousa printing press in Egypt in the year 1894, and copied from a handwritten translation of one of the patriarchs of the East, whose name and interpretation are unknown, and this unknown patriarch took the book from another unknown eastern patriarch as well! This latter book, which translator, interpreter, and publisher are clearly unknown and not endorsed even by any Head of one of the Orthodox Churches, is considered of no more value than that of the rest of the Arabic collections that have been preserved in error and contains obvious errors and distortions by the transcribers and the truncation in the number of the Councils and canons. Therefore, it is not permissible for those who claim to have an education and knowledge, to rely on such unofficial books to prove or refute a fact. Rather, he must resort to official books that are assuredly published,

والمصادق عليها رسمياً والمعترف بها من جميع الكنائس الأرثوذكسية كـكتاب مجموعة جميع قوانين الرسل والمجامع المسكونية والمجامع المكانية وآباء الكنيسة باللغة اليونانية المسمى "بيذاليون" (أي دفّة) والمطبوع بأمر بطريرك ومجمع الكنيسة القسطنطينية والمعترف به من جميع كنائس الشرق الأرثوذكسية". ففي هذا الكتاب - المشروح عنه وعن أهميته مطولاً في كتاب "الكنز الثمين" أيضاً - ترى مجموعة جميع قوانين الرسل والمجامع المكانية التي انعقدت قبل المجامع المسكونية وفى خلالها وتثبتت منها رسمياً، والمجمعين المكانيين الكبيرين اللذين انعقدا في القسطنطينية على إثر المجمع الأخير السابع المسكوني واللذين أثبتنا مختصر تاريخهما في آخر مقالتنا عن "المجامع المقدسة المكانية" وقلنا إن كنيستنا الأرثوذكسية تعتبرهما اعتبار المجامع المكانية التسعة، وأخيراً جميع قوانين الآباء القديسين. فلو تأنَّى صاحب المقالة في "المشرق" قبل كتابته مقالته وبعد اطلاعه على تلك الكتب العربية الأرثوذكسية القليلة المطبوعة والمخطوطة التي، فضلا عن أنه ولا واحد منها يحتوي على قوانين جميع المجامع والآباء القديسين المعتبرة في الكنيسة الأرثوذكسية، لا نرى أيضاً ولا واحداً منها مصادقاً عليه رسمياً - قلنا فلو تأنى وبعث فسألنا من أين أتينا في مجلتنا على كون المجامع المكانية المقدسة هي تسعة وأولها مجمع قرطجنة المنعقد في سنة ٢٥٦ لأجبناه حالاً بإلفات نظره إلى كتاب "البيذاليون" اليوناني المذكور آنفاً طبعته الثانية في أثينا سنة ١٨٤١ الصادرة بأمر بطريرك ومجمع القسطنطينية، حيثما يرى في فهرسته **أولاً** قوانين الرسل الأطهار **ثانياً** قوانين كل مجمع من المجامع السبعة المسكونية وفي جملتها قوانين المجمع المسمى

officially endorsed, and acknowledged by all the Orthodox Churches, such as *The Collection of all the Canons of the Apostles, the Ecumenical Councils, the Local Councils, and the Fathers of the Church* called *Pedalion* in Greek (meaning *The Rudder*) that was printed upon the request of the Patriarch and the Synod of the Church of Constantinople and is acknowledged by all the Orthodox Churches of the East. For in this book—that is described at length in the book *The Precious Treasure* while highlighting its importance—you see the collection of all the Canons of the Apostles and the Local Councils that took place before and during the Ecumenical Councils and that were officially confirmed by them, the two Great Local Councils that took place in Constantinople following the last Seventh Ecumenical Council, whose brief history we confirmed in our last article on "The Holy Local Councils" and we said that our Orthodox Church reckons them as of the same standing as the nine Local Councils, and finally all the canons of the Holy Fathers. Had the author of the article in *Al-Mashreq* proceeded deliberately before writing his article and after examining those few printed and hand-written Arabic Orthodox books—and in addition to the fact that none of them contains the canons of all the Councils and Holy Fathers recognized by the Orthodox Church, and we also do not see any single one of them officially endorsed—we said: had he slowed down and asked us about the origin of our statement in our magazine that the Holy Local Councils are nine (the first of which was the Council of Carthage held in the year 256), we would have answered him immediately by drawing his attention to the aforementioned Greek book *Pedalion*, which second edition was in Athens in the year 1841 upon the request of the Patriarch and the Council of Constantinople, where he would have seen in its index: **first** the canons of the Holy Apostles; **second**, the canons of each of the Seven Ecumenical Councils, including the canons of the Council called the

بالمجمع البنشكتي أي الخامس-السادس المعتبر كتتمة للمجمعين المسكونيين السابقين أي الخامس والسادس اللذين لم يسنّا قوانين تتعلق بنظام الكنيسة وطقوسها. **ثالثاً** قوانين كل من المجامع التسعة المكانية بالترتيب نفسه الذي شرحنا فيه مختصر تاريخ كل منها في مجلتنا تتقدمها قوانين المجمعين المكانيين الكبيرين اللذين انعقدا في القسطنطينية بعد تاريخ المجامع السبعة المسكونية ولهذا ذكرناهما نحن في مجلتنا بعد المجامع التسعة المكانية. **رابعاً** وأخيراً قوانين الآباء القديسين ورسائل بعضهم القانونية التي تعتبرها كنيستنا في عداد قوانينها المقدسة. ولو تأمّل بفهرست القسم الثالث أي بفهرست المجامع المقدسة المكانية المثبتة من مجامع مسكونية لوجد عددها تسعة وفي مقدمتها اسم ضالته المنشودة أي مجمع قرطجنة الذي انعقد تحت رئاسة القديس الشهيد كبريانوس في سنة ٢٥٥-٢٥٦، وبالتالي لأغنانا ونفسه مؤونة الكتابة بهذا الشأن. فالمجامع المقدسة المكانية المثبتة من المجامع المسكونية وهي إذن تسعة، وأولها لأنه أقدمها مجمع قرطجنة سنتي ٢٥٥ و٢٥٦ كما أثبتنا هذا كله في مجلتنا بالتمام طبقاً لما يثبته كتاب "البيذاليون" المعتبر رسميا في جميع الكنائس المسيحية الأرثوذكسية.

ثانياً:

قال صاحب المقالة في "المشرق" إن القانون السابع من قوانين المجمع المسكوني ليس فقط لا يثبت مجمع قرطجنة بل بالحري يخالفه وإن القانون الثاني من قوانين المجمع السادس المسكوني هو من جملة قوانين ليست للمجمع السادس المسكوني لكنها لمجمع القبة الذي ألحقه اليونان سرّاً (!) بالمجمع المسكوني

"Quinisext", i.e., the Fifth-Sixth Council considered as a sequel to the previous Ecumenical Councils, i.e., the fifth and sixth, which did not enact canons related to the Church order and rituals; **third**, the canons of each of the Nine Local Councils, in the same order in which we explained the brief history of each of them in our magazine, preceded by the canons of the two Great Local Councils that were held in Constantinople after the Seven Ecumenical Councils, for which reason we mentioned them in our magazine after the Nine Local Councils; **fourth** and last, the canons of the Holy Fathers and the canonical letters of some of them, which our Church considers amongst her sacred canons. And had he meditated on the index of the third section, i.e., the index of the Holy Local Councils, that were confirmed by Ecumenical Councils, he would have found out that there are nine of them, and at their forefront the name of the object of his quest, i.e., the Council of Carthage, which was presided by the Holy Martyr Cyprian in the year 255-256, and would have therefore spared us and himself the burden of writing in this regard. Hence, the Holy Local Councils confirmed by the Ecumenical Councils are nine, and the first of them is the Council of Carthage for it is the oldest of them, convened in the years 255 and 256, as we have exhaustively proven in our magazine, according to what is proven by the book *Pedalion*, which is officially acknowledged in all the Orthodox Christian churches.

Second:

The author of the article in *Al-Mashreq* said that the seventh canon of the Ecumenical Council does not only disapprove the Council of Carthage, but rather contradicts it, and that the second canon of the Sixth Ecumenical Council's canons, is among the canons that are not part of the Sixth Ecumenical Council, but of the Dome Council (Trullo) that the Greeks secretly added (!) to the Ecumenical

دون اتفاق الآباء ولا تزال الكنيسة الكاثوليكية تنكر قانونيته إذ لم يثبته الأحبار الرومانيون!

فنجيبه على قوله هذا:

يقول شارحو القوانين في كتاب «البيذاليون» ما تعريبه بالحرف الواحد: «ولهذا قد حافظ المجمع الثاني المسكوني في قانونه السابع على هذا القانون الحاضر أي (قانون مجمع قرطجنة) بعض المحافظة. حتى ولو لم يحافظ عليه بتةً لما كان مخالفاً له لأن عمله إنما كان من باب التساهل والتدبير الكنائسي وليس من باب الدقة والصرامة، كما أثبتنا هذا في حاشيتنا على القانون الـ ٤٦ من قوانين الرسل». وأما المجمع السادس المسكوني فقد ثبت قانون مجمع قرطجنة في قانونه الثاني صريحاً، ولئن كان يقول إن العمل بموجبه قد غلب في جهات أفريقية فقط إلا أنه ما دام قد ثبته فقد أيَّده بالحري و لم يبطله. وقد قبل هذا القانون باسيليوس الكبير أيضاً في قانونه الأول (انظر حاشيتنا على القانون الـ ٤٦ من قوانين الرسل).

وهوذا برهان آخر مادامت المجامع المسكونية قد قبلت وثبتت أعمال المجامع المكانية ولا سيما قوانين باسيليوس الكبير كما نظرنا في القانون الثاني للمجمع السادس المسكوني، فتكون أيضاً قد قبلت وثبتت كل القوانين التي سنتها المجامع المكانية وباسيليوس الكبير.

ولزيادة الإيضاح وجوابا على بقية استنتاجات صاحب المقالة في «المشرق» بشأن مسألة **عماد الهراطقة**

Council without the Fathers' agreement and whose can-
onicity is still refuted by the Catholic church, for it wasn't
confirmed by the Roman Popes!

To this we answer him:

The commentators on the canons in the "Pedalion" say
what is literally translated into Arabic as the following:

"That is why the Second Ecumenical Council in its
Canon 7 reserved the present canon apart" i.e. the canon
of the council of Carthage "[but if it did not reserve it for
all, it would not contradict it because][3] it did this by way
of 'economy' and concession, and not with full regard
for accuracy, as we have said in the footnote to Apostolic
Canon 46, and the Sixth Ecumenical Council in its
Canon 2 sanctioned and ratified it even though it may be
said that it applied only to those regions of Africa, yet once
it actually sanctioned and ratified it, it confirmed it still
further, and did not abrogate or annul it. St. Basil the Great,
too, accepts it in his Canon 1. See also the footnote to the
said Apostolic Canon 46."

Another:

"The Ecumenical Council accepted and ratified the
statements of the more particular[4] councils, and indeed by
name the canons of St. Basil the Great, as we saw in Canon 2
of the 6th Ecumenical Council. Hence it is to be logically
inferred that they accepted and confirmed along therewith
everything that the regional councils and Basil the Great
had previously decreed…"

In order to further clarify and answer the rest of the con-
clusions of the article's author in "Al-Mashreq" regarding

3   Square brackets in the quotes are clarifying statments St. Raphael
inserted when quoting the Arabic text of *The Rudder,* but not in *The
Rudder's* English translation.

4   I.e., local councils

نثبت هنا تعريب تفسير القانون الـ ٤٦ من قوانين الرسل مع تعريب الحاشية التي على هذا التفسير المذكورة آنفاً ولكن قبل إثباتنا تعريب التفسير والحاشية نرى مفيداً أن نثبت نص القانون الـ ٤٦ الرسولي الموافق كل الموافقة لقانون مجمع قرطجنة وهذا هو :

نص القانون الرسولي

«أيما أسقف أو قس اقتبل معمودية الهراطقة أو ذبيحتهم نأمر بأن يُقطع لأنه أي اتفاق للمسيح مع بليعال أم أي حظ للمؤمن مع الكافر؟».

تعريب التفسير

يجب على المسيحيين الأرثوذكسيين أن يتجنبوا الهراطقة واحتفالاتهم، بل يجب بالحري على الأساقفة والقسوس أن يوبّخوا الهراطقة وينصحوهم لعلهم يرعوون فيرجعون عن غوايتهم. ولهذا يقول القانون الحاضر إنه أيما أسقف أو قس يقتبل معمودية الهراطقة كصحيحة وحقيقية أو الذبيحة التي تُقدَّم منهم نأمر بأن يُقطع. لأنه أي اتفاق للمسيح مع الشيطان أم أي نصيب للمؤمن مع الكافر (٢ كو ٦:١٥)؟ فإن الذين يقتبلون ما يتمّمه الهراطقة يدلون على كونهم مساهمين لهم بالآراء

the issue of the **Baptism of the Heretics**, we state here the Arabic translation of the interpretation of the Apostolic Canon 46 with the Arabic translation of the footnote on this interpretation mentioned above. But before we state the Arabic translation of the interpretation and the footnote, we find it useful to state the text of the Apostolic Canon 46 that fully agrees with the canon of the Council of Carthage, and it is:

THE TEXT OF THE APOSTOLIC CANON[5]

We order any bishop or priest that has accepted any heretic's baptism or sacrifice to be deposed; for "what concord has Christ with Belial? Or what part has the believer with an unbeliever?"

THE INTERPRETATION'S ARABIC TRANSLATION

It is necessary for us Orthodox Christians to turn away from heretics and the ceremonies of heretics. The heretics ought rather to be rebuked and admonished by bishops and priests in the hope of their apprehending and turning back from their deception. And even more, the present canon prescribes that if any bishop or priest shall accept a heretic's baptism as right and true, or any of their ceremonies,[6] it is ordered that he be deposed. For what concord has Christ with the Devil (cf. II Corinthians 6:15)? Or what portion hath the believer with an unbeliever? Those who accept the

---

5   The following long extract from *The Rudder* is from a new and current working draft of an improved English translation to be published by St. Anthony's Greek Orthodox Monastery. All bold emphasis are from St. Raphael.

6   The translation from the Arabic reads: "or any sacrifice offered by them."

أو على أنهم لا يريدون أن يخلصوهم من الضلال والغواية وفضلاً عن هذا فإن من يرتاح إلى احتفالات الهراطقة كيف يمكنه أن يوبخهم على ضلالهم أو أن يجعلهم ينبذون الهرطقة؟

تعريب الحاشية

من هنا نرى أن القديس الشهيد كبريانوس الذي كان أسقفاً على قرطجنة كما وسائر أعضاء المجمع المؤلف من أربعة وثمانين أسقفاً الذي انعقد تحت رئاسته في قرطجنة بناءً على هذا القانون الرسولي (الـ ٤٦) الذي ينبذ معمودية الهراطقة بل أيضاً على القانون الـ ٦٨- الرسولي الذي يقول بأن الذين يعتمدون أو يتشرطنون من الهراطقة لا يمكن أن يكونوا أو أن يُعتبروا مسيحيين ولا إكليريكيين - قد وضعوا قانونا نبذوا به معمودية الهراطقة والمشاقين أيضاً. وقد استندوا أيضاً في وضعهم هذا القانون إلى شواهد كتابية عديدة ولا سيما إلى قول الرسول القائل: «رب» واحد إيمان واحد. معمودية واحدة» (أف ٤:٥) . فقالوا إذا كانت الكنيسة الجامعة هي واحدة والمعمودية الحقيقية هي واحدة فكيف يمكن أن تكون معمودية الهراطقة والمشاقين حقيقية ما داموا غير باقين داخل الكنيسة الجامعة بل منفصلين عنها بواسطة الهرطقة؟ ولما كانت معمودية الكنيسة الجامعة الأرثوذكسية حقيقية، فإذا اعتبرنا كون معمودية الهراطقة والمشاقين هي أيضاً ،حقيقية، كانت المعمودية ليست واحدة كما يقول بولس الرسول بل اثنتين وهذا فاسد ثم قالوا أيضاً إن عدم قبول معمودية الهراطقة ليس هو رأياً حديثاً بل هو تسليم قويم مرئي الإجراء منذ القديم. وقد تثبت قانون

doings of heretics either themselves entertain similar views to theirs or at any rate they lack an eagerness to free them from their misbelief. For how can those who acquiesce in their ceremonies criticize them with the view of persuading them to give up their misbelief and deceptive[7] heresy?

FOOTNOTE'S ARABIC TRANSLATION

For this reason, too, the ecclesiastic martyr St. Cyprian, who served as bishop of Carthage, and all his synod of eighty-four bishops which had been convoked in Carthage, following the present Apostolic Canon, which simply rejects any baptism of heretics [and schismatics], but also Apostolic Canon 68,[8] which says that those who have been baptized or ordained by heretics… cannot be considered [either Christians or clerics], following, I say, these canons, they laid down a canon whereby they reject the baptism of heretics and of schismatics as well. They prove this by many Scriptural assertions and especially by that of St. Paul the Apostle saying, "One Lord, one faith, one baptism" (Ephesians 4:5). For they say if the Catholic Church is one and the true baptism is one, how can the baptism of heretics and schismatics also be a true baptism at a time when they are not within the Orthodox and Catholic Church [but have been cut off from it as a result of heresy]? But if the baptism of heretics and schismatics is a true baptism, and that of the Orthodox Catholic Church is also a true Baptism, then there is not one Baptism, as St. Paul cries out, but two, which is absurd. And they add this too, that this idea of not accepting a baptism of heretics is not a new or recent one of their own, but on the contrary, an old one and one

---

7   From the Arabic: "cacodoxical and erroneous"

8   St. Raphael says it is from Apostolic Canon 46. The teaching here is also found in Apostolic Canon 68.

مجمع قرطجنة هذا من المجمع السادس المسكوني المقدس في قانونه الثاني وهكذا بعد أن كان قبلا قانون مجمع مكاني خصوصي أصبح قانون مجمع مسكوني لتثبيته من مجمع مسكوني . كذلك نرى أن فرمليانوس الذي ترأس مجمع إيقونية، والذي يسميه باسيليوس الكبير في قانونه الأول «خصيصه» لأنه كان أسقفاً على قيصرية ينبذ أيضاً معمودية الهراطقة وذلك بالتمام مثل القديس كبريانوس ومجمعه لأنه في رسالته إلى القديس كبريانوس يقول: «أي إنسان ولو بلغ أوج الكمال والحكمة يقدر أن يدّعي أو أن يؤمن بأن مجرد استدعاء أسماء الثالوث الأقدس هو الغفران الخطايا ولتقديس المعمودية ما لم يكن أرثوذكسيا هو والذي يعمده؟» (واقرأ رسالته بكاملها الموجودة في كتاب بطاركة أو روشليم كتاب ١، فص ١٦، عدد ٤ ، فإنها ضرورية لهذا الموضوع). كذلك أيضاً باسيليوس الكبير الذي تثبتت قوانينه بكاملها من المجمع السادس المسكوني في قانونه الثاني يوافق مجمع قرطجنة ومجمع فرمليانوس بشأن نبذ معمودية الهراطقة. فإنه حبّاً منه في بيان أية معمودية مقبولة وأية معمودية غير مقبولة قد قسّم المعمودية في قانونه الأول إلى قسمين فقال: «أما **معمودية الهراطقة** أي المنفصلين تماماً عن الكنيسة والمختلفين عن الأرثوذكسيين بالإيمان نفسه والذين اختلافهم يتعلق بالإيمان بالله فقد ارتأى الأقدمون أن **تُنبذ بالكلية.** وأما معمودية المشاقين فقد ارتأى مجمع كبريانوس ومجمع فرمليانوس خصيصاً أن تُنبذ هذه أيضاً، وحجتهم في ذلك أن المشاقين، وأعنى بهم

which has been approved by their predecessors. The canon of this council [of Carthage] was confirmed and ratified by the holy Sixth Ecumenical Council (Canon 2), and from being merely a canon of a local and partial synod it has now become a canon of an Ecumenical Council by reason of its having been confirmed and ratified by the latter [by an Ecumenical Council]. In agreement with St. Cyprian and his council, Firmilian, who served as exarch of the Council in Iconium and whom St. Basil the Great in his first canon calls one of his own, as he was bishop of Caesarea, also invalidates and rejects the baptism of heretics. For in writing to St. Cyprian he writes as follows: "But who, though he has attained to the acme of perfection and of wisdom, can maintain or believe that merely the invocation of the three names of the Holy Trinity is sufficient for the remission of offenses and for the sanctification of the baptism, even when, that is to say, the one baptizing is not an Orthodox?" Read all of his letter that is contained in the chronicle of those who held the office of Patriarch in Jerusalem (Book 1, Chapter 16, page 4), and which is needed in connection with this subject. St. Basil the Great favors this idea, too, whose canons have also been confirmed and ratified by the Sixth Ecumenical Council (Canon 2) [thus agreeing with the Council of Carthage and of Firmilian concerning the baptism of heretics]. For in his first canon, with the intention of saying which baptisms are acceptable and which are unacceptable, he divides them into two classes, stating: "For it appeared to the ancients to be a reasonable rule that **any baptism should be utterly disregarded that has been performed by heretics**, or in other words, by those who have been utterly separated from the Church and who differ from the Orthodox in respect of faith itself, and whose difference is directly dependent on faith in God. As for the baptism of schismatics, on the other hand, it appeared to the council of Cyprian and of my own Firmilian that it too

الكاثريين والأنكراتيين والساكوفوريين والأذروبراستاتيين ومن هم على شاكلتهم بانفصالهم عن الكنيسة قد انفصلت عنهم نعمة الروح القدس وزالت فأصبح رجال إكليروسهم كالعلمانيين لا نعمة روحية فيهم ولا سلطة لهم ليعمدوا أو يشرطنوا وبالتالي أصبح المعمدون منهم كالمعمدين من علمانيين، ولهذا أوجبوا تعميدهم بمعمودية الكنيسة الجامعة الحقيقية. ولكن لما كان البعض من آباء آسيا قد ارتأوا أن تُقبل معمودية المشاقين وذلك من قبيل **التساهل لأجل خلاص الكثيرين منهم فلنقبل**». على أن معمودية المشاقين التي يقبلها باسيليوس الكبير في قانونه الأول هذا من قبيل التساهل يعود هو نفسه فينبذها في قانونه الـ ٤٧ حيث يقول: «أما نحن فنعمد جميع الكاثريين والأنكراتيين والساكوفوريين. ولهذا ولئن كانت إعادة المعمودية ممنوعة عندكم من باب التساهل كما هي ممنوعة عند الرومانيين أيضاً، إلا أنه يجب أن يُعمَل بكلمتنا أي أن تُنبذ معمودية المذكورين». فإذا كان باسيليوس الكبير يريد أن تُنبذ معمودية المشاقين لحرمانهم النعمة المكمِّلة، فليس من حاجة لأن يسأل أحد عما إذا كان يجب تعميد الهراطقة ولا سيما أن باسيليوس الكبير يقول صريحاً في قانونه الأول إن الكنيسة لا تقبل الهراطقة بدون أن تعمّدهم وهذا أيضاً رأي أثناسيوس الكبير الذي قد تثبتت رسائله القانونية من المجمع السادس المسكوني أيضاً في قانونه الثاني. ففي رسالته القانونية الثالثة ضد الأريوسيين يبين براهين قوية كون معمودية الأريوسيين الذين لا يؤمنون إيماناً قويماً بابن يسوع المسيح هي غير حقيقية، وبالتالي يجب تعميدهم كهراطقة. كذلك أيضاً القديس غريغوريوس اللاهوتي في مقالته عن المعمودية يقول إن معمودية الأريوسيين والمكيدونيين الخالين من نعمة: يسوع المسيح ومن نعمة الروح القدس هي غير حقيقية وبالتالي يجب أن

ought to be disregarded and rejected, seeing that the schismatics—the Novatians, the Encratites, the Sakkophores, the Aquarians, and others—have separated in principle from the Church, and after separating have not had the grace of the Holy Spirit in them any longer, as the impartation of it has ceased, thus as having become laymen they have had neither the spiritual gift nor the authority to baptize or to ordain, and consequently those who are baptized by them, as being baptized by laymen, have been ordered to be baptized with the true Baptism of the Orthodox Catholic Church. Yet because it appeared reasonable to some fathers of Asia for the baptism of schismatics to be deemed acceptable **for the sake of some economy in behalf of [the salvation of] the multitude, let it be accepted.**" But note that the baptism of schismatics that he accepts in his first canon, he rejects in his forty-seventh canon, by saying: "In a word, we baptize all Novatians, and Encratites, and Sakkophores. Even if rebaptism is prohibited with you for the sake of some economy as it is with the Romans, nevertheless let our word have the power of rejecting, to put it plainly, the baptism of such." In his first Canon he says decisively that the Church does not accept heretics unless she baptizes them. The same opinion is held by Athanasios the Great whose words were also confirmed and ratified by the Sixth Ecumenical Council [as well as his second canon]....

For he says in his third discourse against the Arians, with strong proofs, that the baptism of Arians, who do not correctly believe in the Son of God Jesus Christ, is not real, therefore they should be baptized as heretics. Moreover, Saint Gregory the Theologian says in his discourse on holy baptism that the baptism of Arians and Macedoniacs, who are devoid of the grace of Jesus Christ and the grace of the Holy Spirit, is not real and therefore they should be baptized as heretics.

يعمدوا كهراطقة. أما القديس يوحنا الذهبي الفم، ففي مقالته على الآية الإنجيلية «في البدء كان الكلمة» يقول: «لا تخدعنك أيها السامع تعاليم الهراطقة، فإنهم وإن يكن عندهم معمودية إلا أنهم ليس عندهم استنارة، فهم بالجسم يتعمدون وأما بالنفس فلا يستنيرون». كذلك القديس لاون يقول في رسالته إلى نيقيطا: «لا يقدر يمنح تقديساً بواسطة الأسرار». وأما أمبروسيوس ففي عظته بشأن الموعوظين يقول : «إن معمودية المنافقين (أي الهراطقة) **لا تقدّس**». وربما ارتاب بعضهم في كيف أن المجمع الثاني المسكوني المقدس في قانونه السابع والمجمع السادس المسكوني المقدس في قانونه الـ ٩٥ لم ينبذ معمودية جميع الهراطقة وفقاً للقوانين الرسولية والمجمع القديس كبريانوس ولسائر الآباء الأماثل العظام المذكورين آنفاً، والذين قد ثبت مؤلفاتهم كما قلنا المجمع السادس المسكوني نفسه في قانونه الثاني بل قد قبلا معمودية البعض الواحد منهم ونبذا معمودية البعض الآخر؟

على أن هذا الارتياب يزول إذا عرفت أن الإدارة أو السياسة في كنيسة المسيح هي على نوعين الواحد يُسمى **الدقة أو الصرامة** والآخَر يُسمى **التدبير أو التساهل** (للضرورة). فالرسل الأطهار وسائر الآباء القديسين الأبرار المذكورين آنها قد اتبعوا في قوانينهم وتعاليمهم المذكورة خطة الدقة والصرامة فرفضوا معمودية الهراطقة بالكلية. وأما آباء المجمعين المسكونيين أي الثاني والسادس فاتبعوا خطة التدبير والتساهل، ولهذا أما معمودية الآريوسيين والمكيدونيين وأمثالهم من الهراطقة فقبلوها، وأما معمودية الأونوميانيين ومن هم على شاكلتهم من الهراطقة فنبذوها، وذلك لأن الآريوسيين والمكيدونيين ولا سيما في زمن

Divine Chrysostom too (in his sermon on "In the beginning was the Word" John 1:1) says the following: "Let not the systems of the heretics fool you, my dear listener: for they have a baptism, but no illumination; accordingly, they are baptized, it is true, with respect to the body, but as respects the soul they are not illuminated." Why, even St. Leo in his epistle to Niketas asserts that "no heretics confer sanctification through the Mysteries" (called "sacraments" in the West). St. Ambrose in his statement concerning catechumens says: "The baptism of the impious **does not sanctify**." In the face of what has been said one might rightfully wonder why the holy 2nd Ecumenical Council in its seventh canon—but still more so why the Sixth Ecumenical in its ninety-fifth canon—failed to disapprove the baptism of all heretics, in accordance with the Apostolic Canons and St. Cyprian's Council and all the other great God-bearing Fathers aforementioned whose writings were confirmed and ratified, as we have said, by the Sixth Ecumenical Council itself in its second canon, whereas, on the contrary, it accepted the baptism of some heretics, but not that of others.

In order to have an easily understandable solution of this perplexity there is need that one should know beforehand that two kinds of government and correction are utilized in the Church of Christ: *Akrivia* and *Oikonomia*. One kind of judgment is called **strictness**[9] (*akrivia*); the other kind is called **economy** (*oikonomia*) [by necessity]... So the fact is that the holy Apostles in their aforesaid canons, and all the saints who have been mentioned, employed strictness, and for this reason they reject the baptism of heretics completely, while, on the other hand, the two Ecumenical Councils employed economy and accepted the baptism of Arians and of Macedoniacs and of others, but refused to recognize that of Eunomians and of still others. Because in the times

9 Or "exactitude"

المجمع الثاني المسكوني كانوا في إبان قوتهم، ليس فقط من حيث كثرة العدد بل أيضاً وبالأكثر من حيث النفوذ لدى ذوي السلطة والرئاسة من الملوك والأمراء وأعضاء مجلس الشيوخ. فالآباء الإلهيون الذين يدبرون كلامهم برشد (مز ١١١: ٥) قد دبروا الأمر على هذا المنوال وتساهلوا بقبول معمودية هؤلاء الهراطقة، أولاً لكي يستميلوهم إلى الأرثوذكسية ويمهدوا لهم طريق الرجوع عن غوايتهم، وثانياً لكي لا يثيروا بالأكثر غضبهم ضد الكنيسة والمسيحيين ويجعلوا الشر أعظم. وشاهدنا أبوا الكنيسة العظيمان باسيليوس وغريغوريوس. فإن الأول خوفاً من أن يهجم محاربو الروح (أي المكيدونيون) على الكنيسة الأرثوذكسية الوحيدة في مدينة قيصرية بما كان لهم وقتئذ من الاقتدار والنفوذ لدى الحكام والولاة عمد إلى خطة التدبير والتساهل، فلبث مدة طويلة لا يسمّي علناً الروح القدس إلها . وأما الثاني فلكي يبيّن قوة الأريوسيين والمكيدونيين الهائلة قال عنهم في خطابه الافتتاحي الذي لفظه أمام آباء المجمع الثاني المسكوني المائة والخمسين ما يأتي: «حقاً إنهم لوحوش ضارية ثائرة على الكنيسة، لأنهم حتى بعد صفاء الجو تراهم لا يرحموننا جاعلين ديدنهم التواقح علينا، إذ لا يزالون حتى الآن أقوى منا». ومعنى هذا أن الأريوسيين والمكيدونيين، مع أن الإمبراطور كان وقتئذ أرثوذكسياً والأرثوذكسية كانت قد انتصرت واعتلنت حتى صار في الإمكان عقد مجمع مسكوني

especially of the 2nd Ecumenical Council, the Arians and the Macedonians were at the height of their influence, and were not only very numerous but also very powerful, and were close to kings, and close to nobles and to the senate. Hence, for one thing, in order to more easily attract them to Orthodoxy and correct them, and for another thing, in order to avoid the risk of infuriating them still more against the Church and the Christians and aggravating the evil[10], those divine Fathers thus managed the matter economically—"managing their words economically with judgment" (Psalm 111:5) and condescended to accept their baptism. That we are not stating this gratuitously and as a matter of mere verbiage, we have ample proof in the testimony of the two great Fathers, St. Basil and St. Gregory. For St. Basil, on the one hand fearing the royal and ruling powers of the Pneumatomachians (i.e., those denying and combating the doctrine of the divinity of the Holy Spirit), and flinching lest they assault the Church of Caesarea, which at that time was the sole bulwark of Orthodoxy, employed economy and for a considerable length of time refrained from openly calling the Holy Spirit God. Gregory the Theologian, on the other hand, wishing to show the powers and the savagery of the Arians and of the Macedonians in the farewell speech he made to the 150 bishops of the 2nd Ecumenical Council itself, told them: "For terrible wild beasts have really fallen upon the Church, and not sparing us after our period of fair weather, but, on the contrary, losing all sense of shame, they are even stronger than the season." Therein he reveals that in spite of the fact that the emperor was an Orthodox Christian, in spite of the fact that Orthodoxy had been preached openly, and an Ecumenical Council had convened

---

10 In the English translation of the Greek is this clarification: "e.g., St. Gregory the Theologian was attacked and stoned by a mob while trying to baptize Arians at the paschal vigil in the spring of 381, the year of the 2nd Ecumenical Council."

ضدهم، كانوا مع هذا كله لا يزالون مخيفين للأرثوذكسية وأقوى من المسيحيين.

قلنا آنفاً إن قبول باسيليوس الكبير معمودية الكاثاريين أي النباطيين (التي قبلها أيضاً المجمعان المسكونيان الثاني والسادس) كان **من قبيل التساهل حباً بخلاص الكثيرين**، ولولا ذلك لكان المجمع السادس مضاداً لنفسه وللمجمع الثاني لأنه قبل معمودية بعض الهراطقة، وفي الوقت نفسه قد ثبت قوانين باسيليوس الكبير الذي في القانون الأول والقانون الـ ٤٧ من قوانينه هذه ينبذ معمودية جميع الهراطقة. فهل يُعقل كون آباء المجمع السادس قد ثبتوا قوانين باسيليوس الكبير بدون أن يقرأوها أو يطلعوا على مضمونها؟ أو لماذا لم يقولوا بأنهم يثبتون كل قوانين باسيليوس الكبير ماعدا الأول والـ٤٧ منها؟ فواضح إذن كون آباء المجمع السادس المسكوني قد أرادوا تفهيمنا أن باسيليوس الكبير قد اتبع خطة الدقة والصرامة، وأما هم وآباء المجمع المسكوين الثاني فقد اتبعوا خطة التدبير والتساهل وبالتالي أنه لا مضادة ولا مناقضة بينهم وبين باسيليوس الكبير.

فمن أهم الأسباب والحالة هذه التي جعلت ذينك المجمعين المسكونيين يقبلان معمودية البعض الواحد من الهراطقة ويرفضان معمودية البعض الآخر هو حب التدبير والتساهل. على أن ثمة سبباً آخر لتصرف هذين المجمعين على هذا المنوال، وهو أن الهراطقة الذين قُبلت معموديتهم كانوا محافظين كل المحافظة على رسم المعمودية الأرثوذكسية ومادتها، فكانوا يتعمّدون بموجب طقس الكنيسة الجامعة الأرثوذكسية. وأما الهراطقة الذين رفضت معموديتهم فكانوا

against them, yet they were still terribly and savagely set against Orthodoxy and were stronger than the Christians.

St. Basil also said in the foregoing that he had accepted the baptism of the Novatians, otherwise called *Katharoi* (which had been accepted by both the Second and the Sixth Ecumenical Councils), merely out of regard **for economy in connection with the [salvation of the] majority of the population**. For had it not been for this ground of economy, how could the Sixth Council have failed to oppose its own action to that of the 2nd Ecumenical Council by itself accepting the baptism of some heretics, yet confirming and ratifying the canons of St. Basil, who in his first and forty-seventh canons utterly refuses to recognize the baptism of heretics? Could it possibly have failed to read the canons of St. Basil itself? Or why should it not have made an exception, and have said that it confirmed and ratified all the other canons of his with the exception of only the first and the forty-seventh? So it is plain that it left it to be understood by us that Basil the Great had employed strictness[11], while, on the contrary, the Second and the Sixth Ecumenical Councils had employed economy; thus there appears to be no contradiction between them.

In fact, this ground of economy is the first and principal reason why those councils accepted the baptism of some heretics and not that of others. In close proximity to the ground of economy there stood also a second reason why they did so. This is due to the fact that those heretics whose baptism they accepted also rigorously observed both the form and the matter of the baptism of the Orthodox, and were willing to be baptized in accordance with the form of the Catholic Church.[12] Those heretics, on the other hand, whose baptism they had refused to recognize, had

11 Or exactitude.
12 I.e., the Orthodox Catholic Church.

قد حرّفوا رسم المعمودية وأفسدوا رتبتها، إما من حيث كلمات
استدعاء الثالوث الأقدس أو من حيث استعمال المادة أي الغطسات
الثلاث. وتؤيّد صحة هذا السبب الآخر كلمات القانون السابع نفسها
للمجمع الثاني المسكوني. وإلا فلماذا قد رفض هذا المجمع معمودية
الأونوميانيين والصابليانيين وقبل معمودية الآريوسيين والمكيدونيين،
في حين أن هؤلاء الأخيرين لم يكونوا بأقل غواية وضلالة من الأولين في
اعتقادهم وتعليمهم عن ابن الله والروح القدس وذلك بحسب شهادة
باسيليوس الكبير وغريغوريوس اللاهوتي وغيرهما؟ فواضح إذن أن
الآريوسيين والمكيدونيين كانوا يتعمّدون بالتمام مثل الأرثوذكسيين
أي بثلاث غطسات وباستدعاء اسم الآب والابن والروح القدس
بدون أن يحرّفوا كلمات الاستدعاء هذه أو يغيّروا شيئاً في استعمال
مادة الماء». وأما الأونوميانيون فقد غيّروا استعمال مادة المعمودية،
إذ كانوا يتعمدون بغطسة واحدة كما تشهد كلمات القانون السابع
للمجمع الثاني المسكوني إذ تقول: «أما الأونوميانيون الذين يعتمدون
بغطسة واحدة والمونطانيون الذين يُسمّون أيضاً فريجيين والصاباليون
الذين أفسدوا رسم المعمودية أي الاستدعاءات الثلاثة معلمين بأن
الآب والابن والروح القدس هم أقنوم واحد..... فنقبلهم كاليونانيين
(أي نعمدهم). أما كون الهراطقة الذين قبل المجمع معموديتهم كانوا
يعتمدون كمعمودية الكنيسة فهذا يؤكده لنا مفسّر القوانين زوناراس

counterfeited the ceremony of baptism and had corrupted the rite or mode of the matter, and the same may be said of the invocations, or use of the matter, and the same may be said of the immersions and emersions.[13] And in proof of the fact that really was the reason we have trustworthy witnesses first in the very words of the seventh canon of the 2nd Ecumenical Council. For what else could have been the reason that it refused to recognize the baptism of the Eunomians and of the Sabellians, while on the other hand, it accepted that of the Arians and of the Macedonians, at a time moreover when Eunomians and Arians and Macedonians were all stubborn heretics? . . . . The evidence is plain that the Arians and the Macedonians, on the one hand, were accustomed to be baptized in precisely the same fashion as were the Orthodox, with three immersions and emersions, and with three invocations of the Holy Trinity, without counterfeiting either the form of the invocations or the matter of the water. . . .

The Eunomians, on the other hand, having counterfeited the mode of baptism, were accustomed to be baptized with only one immersion, as is stated in these same words in the canon, which says, for he is speaking of the Eunomians: "who were accustomed to be baptized with only one immersion" etc., just as the **Sabellians counterfeited the mode of the form of baptism, which is the same as saying that they corrupted the three invocations and taught that the Father and the Son and the Holy Spirit are a single person [we accept them like the Greeks (i.e. we baptize them)].** But that those heretics whose baptism was recognized by the Council were accustomed to be baptized in the form of the baptism of the Church is also borne witness to by Zonaras, interpreter of the canons. For in discussing the seventh canon of the 2nd Ecumenical Council he says verbatim: "These persons

---

13   With reference to Roman Catholics and Protestants.

في شرحه القانون السابع للمجمع الثاني المسكوني إذ يقول: «إن معمودية هؤلاء لا تُعاد لأنها لا تفرق عن معموديتنا بتة بل هي معمودية أرثوذكسية تماماً». وأما كون الهراطقة الذين رفض المجمع قبول معموديتهم ما كانوا يعتمدون كمعمودية الكنيسة فهذا يؤكده لنا زوناراس نفسه أيضاً إذ يقول: «وأما هؤلاء وسائر الهراطقة الآخرين فقد أمر الآباء بأن يعمدوا إما لأنهم لم يحصلوا على المعمودية الإلهية، وإما لأنهم حصلوا عليها ولكن ليس كما يجب أي ليس بحسب ترتيب الكنيسة الأرثوذكسية». فقوانين المجمعين المسكونيين الثاني والسادس قد أمرت بقبول معمودية بعض الهراطقة أولاً لأنهم كانوا محافظين على ترتيب المعمودية الرسولية، وثانياً من قبيل التساهل والتدبير الكنائسي. ولولا هذا الأمر الثاني خصوصاً أي أمر التساهل والتدبير الكنائسي لما كان آباء المجمعين المذكورين يضادون القوانين الرسولية نفسها التي تأمر بالعكس أي بعدم قبول معمودية الهراطقة إجمالاً.

ثم إن الحاشية تسترسل بعد ذلك في الكلام عن معمودية اللاتين في عصرنا الحاضر مما نغفل ذكره مكتفين بما أوردناه منها آنفاً كبيان كاف للموضوع الذي نحن بصدده.

والخلاصة

إن كنيستنا القويمة الأرثوذكسية الرأي المشهورة بمحافظتها الشديدة على تسليم الرسل القديم

therefore, are not rebaptized, because as respects Holy Baptism they differ in nothing from us, but are accustomed to be baptized exactly the same as are the Orthodox." But that those heretics whose baptism was not recognized by the council, were not accustomed to be baptized in the same form as the Baptism of the Church, is borne witness to again by the same Zonaras, who says: "As for these and all other heretics, the Holy Fathers have decreed that they be baptized. For whether they received divine Baptism or not, they have not received it correctly, nor in the form prescribed by the Orthodox Church."

So because of the fact that those heretics were accustomed to observe the form of apostolic baptism, the canons of those two Councils accepted them as baptized persons, yet not for this reason alone, but also for the sake of economy, as we have said. For if economy had not been at stake, they certainly would not have flown in the face of the Apostolic Canons which command the contrary—that is to say, that we must not recognize or accept the baptism of heretics.

Then the footnote goes on to talk about the baptism of the Latins in our present time which we do not discuss here, we resolve [this issue] with what we mentioned above as a sufficient statement of the subject with which we are dealing.[14]

CONCLUSION

Our Orthodox Church, who is well-known for its strict preservation of what the ancient Apostles handed down and of the direct teaching of the Fathers and Ecumenical Councils, has followed and continues following the path of a

14 St. Nikodemos goes on to explain in his commentary that the Latins must be received by baptism since they are heretics and they had ceased to practice the canonical form of baptism.

وتعليم الآباء والمجامع المسكونية القويم كانت ولا تزال تجري في مسألة عماد الهراطقة والمشاقين مجرى المدبّر الروحي الحكيم. ففي الأماكن والبلاد التي تأمن فيها شرهم وتؤمل امكانية استمالة كثيرين منهم إلى الأرثوذكسية تجري على خطة التساهل والتدبير الكنائسي، فنقبل معمودية أولئك منهم الذين يتممونها قانونيا باسم الآب والابن والروح القدس، كما تفعل الآن الكنيسة الأرثوذكسية الروسية مع اللاتين وبعض الجماعات البروتسطانية في بلادها حين اتحادهم بالكنيسة الأرثوذكسية وأما في الأماكن والبلاد التي تخشى فيها وقاحتهم وشرورهم وتحرشاتهم بها ولا أمل لها بإمكانية استمالتهم إلى الأرثوذكسية فتجري على خطة الدقة والصرامة معهم فلا تقبل معموديتهم كما هو الجاري الآن في جميع البطريركيات الأرثوذكسية وسائر الكنائس الأرثوذكسية اليونانية.

wise spiritual steward in the matter of baptizing heretics and schismatics. In places and countries where she feels safe from their evil, and hopes that many of them can be attracted to Orthodoxy, she follows a plan of leniency and ecclesiastical economy, so she accepts the baptism of those among them who complete it canonically[15] in the name of the Father, the Son, and the Holy Spirit, as the Russian Orthodox Church is now doing with the Latins and some Protestant groups in her country when they unite with the Orthodox Church. But in places and countries where she fears their insolence, evils, and harassment, and has no hope of the possibility of attracting them to Orthodoxy, she follows a plan of accuracy and exactitude with them, so she does not accept their baptism, as is the case now in all Orthodox Patriarchates and all other Greek Orthodox churches.[16]

---

15 In the text he quoted from *The Rudder*, St. Raphael clearly understood that for baptism to be performed "canonically" it must be done in three immersions in the name of the Holy Trinity.

16 There is an apparent contradiction between the application of economy by Saint Nikodemos in *The Rudder* (stated as authoritative "by the entire Orthodox Church") and in Saint Raphael's article. After St. Raphael's excerpted and lengthy quotation from *The Rudder*, St. Nikodemos explains that certain heretics who maintained the apostolic form of baptism (three immersions in the name of the Holy Trinity) were permitted by the Ecumenical Councils to be received by economy because of their terrible savagery against the Orthodox and the concern that if the Church requires they undergo baptism then this might incite them to vicious violence against the Orthodox. This divergence could have a few explanations, including: (1) There may be confusion with the Russian Church on these matters brought on by the 1666-1667 Moscow Council (see *On the Reception of the Heterodox into the Orthodox Church: The Patristic Consensus and Criteria*, pp. 45-56 and chapters 9 and 11-13). St. Raphael may have believed that the Russian Church only accepted Latins and Protestants by economy if they had maintained the canonical form of baptism in three immersions. St. Raphael possibly did not understand by his time Russia had ceased mandating the patristic consensus of a canonical form of baptism as a require-

St. Nikodemos the Hagiorite

ment for the applying of economy. (2) There may be need to look at this from the point of view of historical context. While the savagery of the Arians and Macedonians against the Church, referred to in *The Rudder*, was physical and material in nature, the harassment of the Latins (Jesuits, Maronites, etc.) was spiritual and dogmatic in nature during the times of Saint Raphael, i.e., their publications attacked Orthodox teachings as he shows in the article above. Also the proselytism that both Latins and Protestants exercised in the Church of Antioch since the 17th century was aggressive. Perhaps, Saint Raphael wanted to counter such spiritual persecution with more rigor in the application of the canons when receiving the heterodox of that period of time in the life of the Church. Despite these opposing positions, St. Raphael and St. Nikodemos agree that those heretics who retained the canonical form could be received by economy, if necessary.

The Twelve Apostles

APPENDIX[1]

Such being the case, it now remains for us to also point out that rich storehouse in which the Apostles, according to St. Irenaeus, "deposited all things of truth." In other words, it remains for us to examine which of the two Churches already divided and in conflict, I speak of the Eastern and the Western, is the true treasury and certain protection of sacred Traditions. The papist Church, which separated from the one, holy, catholic, and apostolic Orthodox Church of Christ through condemnations, which the Lord knows, confidently asserts that the apostolic Church of Rome is a true treasury of the truly apostolic Traditions; the infallible representative of Christ on earth, the key-keeping Pope, is the faithful guardian of them! (see Heinrich Klee, *Lehrbuch der Dogmengeschichte*, "Concerning Tradition," § 2). But if one might open the impartial history of the Church, it will be observed that the Western Church that walked together modestly and steadfastly with the Eastern Church until about the ninth century, which [the Western Church]

---

1   Excerpt from "The True Significance of Sacred Tradition and Its Great Worth" by St. Raphael of Brooklyn, translated by Father Patrick Demetrios Viscuso, pp. 57-62.

certainly, according to the witness of Sozomen, "regulating
itself purely by the doctrines of the Fathers, wished to avoid
quarrels and prattle concerning these things" (*Church History*
3.127), from that time, because it no longer prospered, by
the conceit of Lucifer becoming arrogant, inasmuch as
viewing itself as more senior among equal sisters, and di-
verging from the royal road that up to then it walked along,
it took the one leading to innovations, making use of every
means licit and illicit in order that it might also drag the
chaste sister, the Eastern Church, with it into the abyss of
false belief into which it had fallen! In this manner, propor-
tionately to her ambitious proclivities, advancing from error
to error in spiritual and worldly affairs, it has left nothing
unshaken, nothing without innovation, nothing without
perversion—neither doctrines, nor mysteries, nor customs—but it spoiled and distorted everything written and
unwritten! In truth, time lacks even to simply enumerate the
shameless innovations of the papist Church, which both
church and civil history report with horror, but lest I appear
to say unsubstantiated things, let it be permitted for me that
I make a brief comparison of the present-day so-called papist Church with our Orthodox Church, or rather with itself,
when at one time, being in agreement in everything with
our own Church, it was called an orthodox Church of
Rome, because nothing more disinterested and impartial
than history can demonstrate for us which of the two dis-
cussed Churches is the faithful and true guardian of sacred
Traditions. And first, when studying the history of church
hierarchy, we see that whereas the ancient Roman Church
viewed the bishop of Rome as simply a spiritual and only an
administrative leader of the West, the papist Church views
him as both an absolute spiritual and worldly leader of
Christianity as a whole, contrary to both Scripture (Mt.
20:26; Lk. 22:26) and Tradition (First Ecumenical Council, canon 6). Whereas the ancient Roman Church viewed

the hierarch of Rome as *primus inter pares* (= first among equals) and as subject to the decisions of ecumenical councils, to which also the Apostle Peter submitted himself (Gal. 2:11), the papist Church views him as *summus pontifex* (= supreme hierarch) and, when placed above the councils, honors and venerates him as the infallible (oh the folly!) representative (!) of God upon earth, contrary both to Scripture (Mt. 20:26, 27; Eph. 2:20) and Tradition (Apostolic Canon 34; First Ecumenical Council, canon 6; Second Ecumenical Council, 2 and 4; Sixth [Ecumenical Council], 36; etc.). (Compare Φ. Βαφείδης, *Ἐκκλησιαστικὴ Ἱστορία*, vol. 2, § 130.) But second, let us also open the history of divine doctrines and mysteries and let us see if the papist Church feared these. But alas! The papacy also overturned these things because whereas the orthodox Roman Church taught that the Holy Spirit proceeds from the Father while anathematizing any addition or subtraction in the Symbol of Faith, the papist Church not only teaches the *Filioque* (= and from the Son), but also adds it in the Symbol of Faith (see Φ. Βαφείδης, *Ἐκκλησιαστικὴ Ἱστορία*, vol. 2, § 130) contrary to Scripture (Jn. 55:268) and Tradition (all of the ecumenical councils and all of the Fathers of the Western and Eastern Church until the ninth century). Whereas the orthodox Roman Church celebrated baptism by triple immersion, the papist one introduced infusion and sprinkling, contrary both to Scripture (Mk. 1:10; Acts 8:36-39; Rom. 6:4; Col. 2:12) and Tradition (Apostolic Canon 50; Second Ecumenical Council, 7; Sixth, 45; paradoxically, also compare Klee, *Dogmatik*, 3:129). Whereas the orthodox Roman Church immediately after holy baptism celebrated the mystery of chrismation, the papist one celebrates it not just by the bishop alone, but also after the child reaches seven to twelve years of age, calling it *confirmatio* (= confirmation), contrary both to Scripture (Acts 8:14-17; 19:2-6) and Tradition (Council of Laodicea, canon 48; Dionysius the Areopagite,

Ecclesiastical Hierarchy 7; Cyril of Jerusalem, *Catechetical Lecture* 18.33). Whereas the orthodox Roman Church celebrated the divine Eucharist with leavened bread, the papist one celebrates it with unleavened, contrary both to Scripture (Mt. 26:26; Mk. 14:22; Lk. 24:30-35; Jn. 6:35, 41, 48, 51, 58; Acts 2:42-46; 20:7; 1 Cor. 10:16; 11:20) and Tradition (Justin, *Apology* 1.66; Irenaeus, *Against Heresies* 4.18; Cyril of Jerusalem, *Mystagogic Catechesis* 4.1-6; Ambrose, *On the Sacrament of the Incarnation of the Lord* 4.4). Whereas the orthodox Roman Church invoked God that He might hallow the offered gifts when blessing them with the sign of the Cross, the papist one recites simply and historically the words of institution ("this is My body" and "this is My blood"), being of the opinion that by them and by only displaying the holy gifts, they are hallowed and transubstantiated, contrary clearly to apostolic and divine Tradition (see the Liturgy of the Apostle James and in general the ancient liturgies of the Orthodox; and compare also Irenaeus, *Against Heresies* 4.24; Origen, *Against Celsus* 8; Cyril of Jerusalem, *Mystagogic Catechesis* 1.7, 3.3, 5.7; Basil, *Concerning the Holy Spirit* 27; Augustine, *On the Trinity* 3.4; etc.). Finally, whereas the orthodox Roman Church provided this fearful mystery to all the faithful without exception and under both species, the papist one not only deprived small children of it contrary to apostolic Tradition (Apostolic Constitutions 8.13; Dionysius the Areopagite, *Ecclesiastical Hierarchy* 7.11: Cyprian, *Testimonies against the Jews* 3.25; Augustine, *On the Merits and Remission of Sins and on the Baptism of Infants* 1.20; and others), but also dared to exclude all the laity from communion of the precious blood of Christ, contrary both to Scripture (which expressly commands, "Drink of it, all of you" [Mt. 26:27; Mk. 14:23]) and Tradition (all of the seven ecumenical councils and ancient Fathers of the Church). Whereas the orthodox Roman Church viewed the penances imposed in the mystery of repentance as having a simple correcting

effect on the one repenting, the papist one, misunderstand-
ing the true meaning of this mystery, not only subdivided it
into three, namely, into *contritionem* (= contrition), *confessionem*
(= confession), and *satisfactionem* (= satisfaction), but also
views the penances as having an effect propitiatory of the
divine justice that is offended by the sin of the one repenting,
and as if this did not suffice, it added, on the one hand, that
by virtue of the authority given to it from God to bind and
loose, it can release from these penances the one repenting
through pardoning absolutions, which are bestowed from
the inexhaustible treasury that it possesses of excess merits
earned not only by Christ, but also the saints (!!!); and on the
other hand, that these absolutions work even after death to
emancipate the one who happened to die under the burden
of penances from the punishment of purifying fire (!!!). The
papist Church teaches all these things contrary both to
Scripture (Lk. 15:18, 19; 18:13; 2 Cor. 7:10; 1 Pt. 4:8;
Acts 10:43; 4:12; Heb. 7:25) and Tradition (Cyprian, *On
the Lapsed* 30; Basil, *On Isaiah* 15; John Chrysostom,
Homily on 2 Tim. 6.3). But let us proceed further: whereas
the orthodox Roman Church prescribed celibacy as
obligatory only for bishops (according to canon 12 of the
Ecumenical Council in Trullo), the papist one imposed
it on all clergy in general, both great and small, contrary
both to Scripture (Eph. 5:31-32; 1 Tim. 4:3)
and Tradition (Apostolic Canon 5; Sixth Ecumenical,
canons 13 and 18; Carthage, 4 and 33; Gangra, 1, 4, and 14).
Whereas the orthodox Roman Church permitted the
dissolution of marriage in the case of spousal infidelity,
the papist one views it as completely indissoluble, contrary both to Scripture (Mt. 5:32) and Tradition
(Neocaesarea, canon 8; Carthage, 115; Basil,
canons 9, 21, 39, and 48; Sixth, canon 87). Finally,
whereas the orthodox Roman Church celebrated unction
both by priests and for any sick [person] whatsoever, the

papist one celebrates it only by the bishop and only for those who are dying as a last anointing (= *extrema unctio*), contrary both to Scripture (Jas. 5:14, 15) and Tradition (Chrysostom, *Concerning the Priesthood* 3.6; Cyril of Alexandria, *Encomium on Holy Mary the Theotokos* 6.13). In general, regarding these innovations of the papist Church concerning the mysteries, see Φ. Βαφείδης, Ἐκκλησιαστικὴ Ἱστορία, vol. 2, § 192 and § 194; Δημήτριος Βερναρδάκης, Ἱερὰ Κατήχησις, "Concerning the Mysteries"; and Γρηγόριος, Ἡ φωνὴ τῆς Ὀρθοδοξίας. But after these doctrines and mysteries had finally undergone such change and alteration in the papist Church, what must one understand regarding the other apostolic and church customs? Perhaps papism left these undisturbed? Not at all, because whereas the orthodox Church of Rome forbade fasting or kneeling on the Sabbath, breaking the fast on Wednesday or Friday, eating blood or clotted blood or any other impure thing, using any musical instrument whatsoever in the churches, venerating statues or unwritten images, ordaining more than one priest during one and the same liturgy, offering every day more than one sacrifice on the same altar, shaving hair or the beard and much more the mustache—whereas, I say, all these things and many such others, on account of good order and decorum, the ancient orthodox Church of Rome forbade, as identically the ortho-dox Eastern Church does up to the present day, on the other hand, the papist Church does not only simply allow all these things, but also imposes strictly many of them, completely contrary to the purely apostolic and church Tradition of which was decreed, "Let the ancient customs prevail" (First Ecumenical Council, canon 6). In general, concerning such innovations of the papist Church, see Εὐγένιος Βούλγαρης, Κατὰ Λατίνων Στηλιτευτικὴ Ἐπιστολή; Γρηγόριος, Ἡ φωνὴ τῆς Ὀρθοδοξίας; and Πηδάλιον. Consequently, after also explaining such things of papism, let any impartial man tell us which of the two said Churches is the true treasury and certain protection of sacred Traditions, or as Irenaeus said, "the rich storehouse in which the Apostles have deposited all things of truth": the papist Church, which innovated so much and greatly from 1054 until the present day, or the orthodox Eastern Church, which neither added or subtracted nor altered a jot or tittle from the divine deposit handed over to it from apostolic times until the present day?

St. Raphael of Brooklyn

UNCUT MOUNTAIN PRESS TITLES

Books by Archpriest Peter Heers

Fr. Peter Heers, *The Ecclesiological Renovation of Vatican II: An Orthodox Examination of Rome's Ecumenical Theology Regarding Baptism and the Church*, 2015

Fr. Peter Heers, *The Missionary Origins of Modern Ecumenism: Milestones Leading up to 1920*, 2007

The Works of our Father Among the Saints, Nikodemos the Hagiorite

Vol. 1: *Exomologetarion: A Manual of Confession*

Vol. 2: *Concerning Frequent Communion of the Immaculate Mysteries of Christ*

Vol. 3: *Confession of Faith*

Other Available Titles

Elder Cleopa of Romania, *The Truth of our Faith*

Elder Cleopa of Romania, *The Truth of our Faith, Vol. II*

Fr. John Romanides, *Patristic Theology: The University Lectures of Fr. John Romanides*

Demetrios Aslanidis and Monk Damascene Grigoriatis, *Apostle to Zaire: The Life and Legacy of Blessed Father Cosmas of Grigoriou*

Protopresbyter Anastasios Gotsopoulos, *On Common Prayer with the Heterodox According to the Canons of the Church*

Robert Spencer, *The Church and the Pope*

G. M. Davis, *Antichrist: The Fulfillment of Globalization*

Athonite Fathers of the 20ᵗʰ Century, Vol. I

St. Gregory Palamas, *Apodictic Treatises on the Procession of the Holy Spirit*

St. Hilarion Troitsky, *On the Dogma of the Church*

Fr. Alexander Webster and Fr. Peter Heers, Editors, *Let No One Fear Death*

Subdeacon Nektarios Harrison, *Metropolitan Philaret of New York*

Elder George of Grigoriou, *Catholicism in the Light of Orthodoxy*

Archimandrite Ephraim Triandaphillopoulos, *Noetic Prayer as the Basis of Mission and the Struggle Against Heresy*

Dr. Nicholas Baldimtsis, *Life and Witness of St. Iakovos of Evia*

On Reception of the Heterodox into the Orthodox Church

Patrick (Craig) Truglia, *Rise and Fall of the Papacy*

Select Forthcoming Titles

Orthodox Patristic Witness Concerning Catholicism

George Pachymeres, *Errors of the Latins*

Fr. Peter Heers, *Going Deeper in the Spiritual Life*

Athonite Fathers of the 20ᵗʰ Century, Vol. II

This 1ˢᵗ Edition of

IN DEFENSE OF SAINT CYPRIAN
WITH REFERENCE TO ST. NIKODEMOS
AND *THE RUDDER*

written by St. Raphael of Brooklyn and printed in this two thousand twenty third year of our Lord's Holy Incarnation is one of the many fine titles available from Uncut Mountain Press, translators and publishers of Orthodox Christian theological and spiritual literature. Find the book you are looking for at

u n c u t m o u n t a i n p r e s s . c o m

**GLORY BE TO GOD
FOR ALL THINGS**

A M E N.

Printed in the USA
CPSIA information can be obtained
at www.ICGtesting.com
LVHW071002200724
786056LV00038B/1654